ON THE COVER

Researchers crossing the Loch to collect wet deposition samples from the NADP/NTN monitoring site at Rocky Mountain National Park.
Credit: U.S. Geologic Survey.

ON THIS PAGE

View looking northeast toward the Loch from Andrews Tarn.
Credit: U.S. Geologic Survey.

2009 Monitoring and Tracking Wet Nitrogen Deposition at Rocky Mountain National Park

September 2011

Natural Resource Report NPS/NRSS/ARD/NRR—2011/ 442

Kristi Morris
National Park Service, Air Resources Division

Alisa Mast
Dave Clow
U.S. Geological Survey, Rocky Mountain Region, Colorado Water Science Center

Greg Wetherbee
U.S. Geological Survey, Branch of Quality Systems, NADP External QA Project

Jill Baron
U.S. Geological Survey, Colorado State University—Natural Resource Ecology Laboratory

Curt Taipale
Colorado Department of Public Health and Environment, Air Pollution Control Division

Tamara Blett
National Park Service, Air Resources Division

David Gay
NADP Program Officer, Program Coordinator

Eric Richer
Colorado State University—Natural Resource Ecology Laboratory

September 2011

U.S. Department of the Interior
National Park Service
Natural Resource Stewardship and Science
Denver, Colorado

The National Park Service, Natural Resource Stewardship and Science office in Denver, Colorado publishes a range of reports that address natural resource topics of interest and applicability to a broad audience in the National Park Service and others in natural resource management, including scientists, conservation and environmental constituencies, and the public.

The Natural Resource Report Series is used to disseminate high-priority, current natural resource management information with managerial application. The series targets a general, diverse audience, and may contain NPS policy considerations or address sensitive issues of management applicability.

All manuscripts in the series receive the appropriate level of peer review to ensure that the information is scientifically credible, technically accurate, appropriately written for the intended audience, and designed and published in a professional manner. This report received formal, high-level peer review based on the importance of its content, or its potentially controversial or precedent-setting nature. Peer review was conducted by highly qualified individuals with subject area technical expertise and was overseen by a peer review manager.

Views, statements, findings, conclusions, recommendations, and data in this report do not necessarily reflect views and policies of the National Park Service, U.S. Department of the Interior. Mention of trade names or commercial products does not constitute endorsement or recommendation for use by the U.S. Government.

This report is available from the Air Resources Division of the NPS (www.nature.nps/air/pubs/pdf/rmnp-trends/rmnp-trends_2009.pdf) and the Natural Resource Publications Management Web site (http://www.nature.nps.gov/publications/nrpm) on the Internet.

Please cite this publication as:

National Park Service, Air Resources Division. 2011. 2009 monitoring and tracking wet nitrogen deposition at Rocky Mountain National Park: September 2011. Natural Resource Report NPS/NRSS/ARD/NRR—2011/442. National Park Service, Denver, Colorado.

NPS 121/109707, September 2011

Contents

Tables

Figures

Acknowledgements

The authors acknowledge Chris Lehmann, Mark Rhodes, Jim Cheatham, and Lisa Clarke for their participation in numerous scientific discussions regarding the tracking of nitrogen deposition data. The authors thank Kristi Gebhart and George Ingersoll for assisting with the statistical analyses. The authors also thank John Vimont, Susan Johnson, Doug Druliner, Kathy Tonnessen, and Mark Nilles for their careful review of the report. Any use of trade, product, or firm names is for descriptive purposes only and does not imply endorsement by the U.S. Government

1. Background Information on the Nitrogen Deposition Reduction Plan

In 2004, a multi-agency meeting including the Colorado Department of Public Health and Environment (CDPHE), the National Park Service (NPS), and the U.S. Environmental Protection Agency (EPA) was held to address the effects and trends of nitrogen deposition and related air quality issues at Rocky Mountain National Park (RMNP). These agencies signed a Memorandum of Understanding (MOU) to facilitate interagency coordination, calling the effort the "Rocky Mountain National Park Initiative." After much collaboration, the MOU agencies (CDPHE, NPS, and EPA) issued the Nitrogen Deposition Reduction Plan (NDRP) in 2007, which was endorsed by the three agencies and the Colorado Air Quality Control Commission (AQCC). The NDRP and other related documents are available on the CDPHE website, http://www.cdphe.state.co.us/ap/rmnp.html.

As part of the NDRP, the NPS adopted and the MOU agencies endorsed 1.5 kilograms of nitrogen per hectare per year (kg N/ha/yr) wet deposition as an appropriate science-based threshold for identifying adverse ecosystem effects in RMNP. This threshold is based on decades of research and is the "critical load" of nitrogen that can be absorbed by ecosystems within RMNP before detrimental changes occur (Baron et al. 2006). To achieve this threshold, referred to as the resource management goal (RMG), the MOU agencies have chosen a glidepath approach. This type of approach anticipates gradual improvement over time and is a commonly used regulatory structure for long-term, goal-oriented air quality planning.

The glidepath approach allows for the RMG for RMNP to be met over the course of 25 years. The baseline condition at Loch Vale in RMNP is 3.1 kg N/ha/yr. The first interim milestone requires a reduction of wet nitrogen deposition from baseline conditions to 2.7 kg N/ha/yr by the year 2012. Progress towards this and subsequent interim milestones will be assessed using the weight of evidence at 5 year intervals starting in 2013 until the RMG is achieved in the year 2032. The weight of evidence approach uses multiple types of information in the decision making process. Further explanation is provided in Section 5 of this report.

The NDRP required that a Contingency Plan be developed to put in place corrective measures in the event that the initial 2013 milestone and any subsequent interim milestones are not achieved. The Nitrogen Deposition Data Tracking Plan was included as Appendix B of the Contingency Plan (http://www.cdphe.state.co.us/ap/rmnp/RMNPContingencyPlanFinal.pdf). The MOU agencies will work together each year to update the analyses

Subalpine meadow ecosystems are sensitive to the effects of nutrient enrichment from atmospheric deposition.
Credit: National Park Service.

used to track nitrogen deposition at the park with the most recently available data. A report similar to this one will be peer-reviewed and published annually by the NPS.

The MOU agencies will meet by September of each year to discuss the analyses and determine whether the Contingency Plan should be revised based on new information. In the years following the interim milestones (and within 180 days of the issuance of the deposition data), the MOU agencies will evaluate how nitrogen deposition is changing at RMNP and determine whether an interim milestone was achieved. If the agencies concur that a milestone was not achieved, the contingency process will be triggered.

2. Purpose

The purpose of this report is to inform the MOU agencies, stakeholders, and the public about the current status and trends of wet nitrogen deposition at RMNP. In addition to other information, the MOU agencies will use the information provided in this report to make a determination of whether the interim milestones have been achieved in 2013, 2018, 2023, and 2028.

3. Monitoring Wet Nitrogen Deposition

The RMG and interim milestones identified in the NDRP are based on wet nitrogen (N)[1] deposition data at Loch Vale in RMNP that are collected through the National Atmospheric Deposition Program/National Trends Network (NADP/NTN). The NADP/NTN is a nationwide precipitation chemistry monitoring network and a cooperative effort between many different groups, including the U.S. Geological Survey, EPA, NPS, U.S. Department of Agriculture, State Agricultural Experiment Stations, and numerous other universities, governmental and private entities. The NADP/NTN began monitoring in 1978 with 22 sites but grew rapidly in the early 1980s. Much of the expansion occurred during the implementation of monitoring under the National Acid Precipitation Assessment Program. Today the network has almost 250 sites spanning the continental U.S., Alaska, Puerto Rico, and the Virgin Islands.

The purpose of the network is to collect data and monitor geographical patterns and long-term trends in precipitation chemistry. The precipitation at each site is collected weekly according to strict clean-handling procedures. It is then sent to the NADP Central Analytical Laboratory in Champaign, IL, where it is analyzed for hydrogen (acidity as pH), specific conductance, sulfate, nitrate, ammonium, chloride, calcium, magnesium, potassium, and sodium. Stringent quality assurance and quality control programs ensure that the data are accurate and precise. More information on these programs and the monitoring data can be found on the NADP/NTN website at http://nadp.isws.illinois.edu. Annual data are generally available on the website six months after completion of the calendar year.

NADP/NTN data are used widely in publications, including nearly 150 peer-reviewed journal articles in 2010. Data are also used extensively by the EPA to assess progress made by the Acid Rain Program, which seeks to reduce emissions of sulfur dioxide (SO_2) and nitrogen oxides (NO_X). The most recent report, "Acid Rain and Related Programs: 2009 Highlights" is available at http://www.epa.gov/airmarkt/progress/ARP09.htm.

Wet deposition collector at Loch Vale in Rocky Mountain NP.
Credit: National Park Service.

4. Monitoring in Rocky Mountain NP

There are two NADP/NTN sites in RMNP. The Loch Vale site is located at a high elevation of 3,159 m and the Beaver Meadows site is located at a lower elevation of 2,490 m. Both sites have been operating since the early 1980s. Data from the Loch Vale site are the primary focus of the NDRP because the RMG of 1.5 kg N/ha/yr wet deposition is based on NADP/NTN data from this site. The RMG was set to protect the most sensitive resources in the park which are also at the highest elevations.

Routine monitoring in a remote, high elevation location presents several challenges. The samples from Loch Vale are collected each week by a dedicated site operator who hikes or skis in 5 km (approximately 3 miles) to the monitoring site year-round. Missed samples sometimes result from equipment issues and/or inadequate solar power supply during the harsh winter months. Due to the importance of these data in tracking deposition, the MOU agencies agreed to co-locate a second set of NADP/NTN monitoring equipment at Loch Vale, which was installed in September of 2009. At that time, the site included two precipitation collectors, two electronic rain gages, and the original rain gage for comparison. Over the last year, solar panels and batteries were upgraded to ensure adequate power supply and storage. Telemetry was also added to the site to allow equipment and/or power issues to be identified quickly and resolved during the following weekly site visit. These modifications have enhanced reliability. Appendices A and B provide a history of the Loch Vale monitoring site and a comparison of the rain gages.

[1] The nitrogen measured by NADP/NTN is inorganic, and all references to wet nitrogen deposition in this report refer to the inorganic portion of nitrogen deposition only.

5. Tracking Wet Nitrogen Deposition at Rocky Mountain NP

The interim milestones in the NDRP are based on a 5 year rolling average of the annual wet nitrogen deposition data from the Loch Vale NADP/NTN site in RMNP (http://nadp.sws.uiuc.edu/sites/siteinfo.asp?id=CO98&net=NTN). The first interim milestone of the NDRP calls for this 5 year rolling average of wet nitrogen deposition at the park to be reduced from the baseline loading of 3.1 in 2006 to 2.7 kg N/ha/yr in 2012. Another goal of the NDRP is to "reverse the trend of increasing nitrogen deposition at the park." Determination of the success or failure of the goals of the NDRP will be determined by the weight of evidence. Several analyses will be used to track nitrogen deposition at RMNP. These analyses may be modified as better information becomes available and will include, but are not limited to the following: (1) assessment of progress along the glidepath, (2) long-term trend analyses for RMNP and other regional sites, and (3) short-term trend analyses for RMNP and other regional sites. Each section below describes the details of the analyses and shows results for the analyses ending in 2009.

5.1. Assessment of progress along the glidepath

This assessment compares current wet nitrogen deposition (calculated as the most recent 5 year average) at the original Loch Vale NADP/NTN site to the interim milestones on the NDRP glidepath. Annual wet nitrogen deposition is calculated by multiplying the annual precipitation-weighted mean nitrogen concentration by the annual amount of precipitation (see Appendix C for explanation of NADP/NTN terms and calculations). Therefore, deposition values are influenced by wet years and dry years. Using the 5 year average of wet nitrogen deposition reduces the inter-annual variability caused by precipitation.

Figure 1 shows the glidepath from the NDRP. The first interim milestone is 2.7 kg N/ha/yr of wet deposition in 2012, followed by three more interim milestones at 5 year intervals, eventually resulting in a wet deposition of 1.5 kg N/ha/yr and achievement of the resource management goal in 2032. The estimate for nitrogen deposition under natural conditions, 0.2 kg N/ha/yr is also shown in Figure 1 (Galloway et al. 1995 and 1996; Dentener 2001).

The glidepath model allows us to answer the question: Is current wet nitrogen deposition in RMNP on or below the glidepath? Current wet nitrogen deposition (5 year rolling average) is shown in red (depicted in Figure 1) for 2006 through 2009. In 2009, the calculated 5 year average (2005–2009) of wet nitrogen deposition was 3.0 kg N/ha/yr. This value represents a 0.1 kg N/ha/yr departure from the glidepath (green line depicted in Figure 1). Therefore, the answer to the question is: no, wet nitrogen deposition is not on or below the glidepath in 2009.

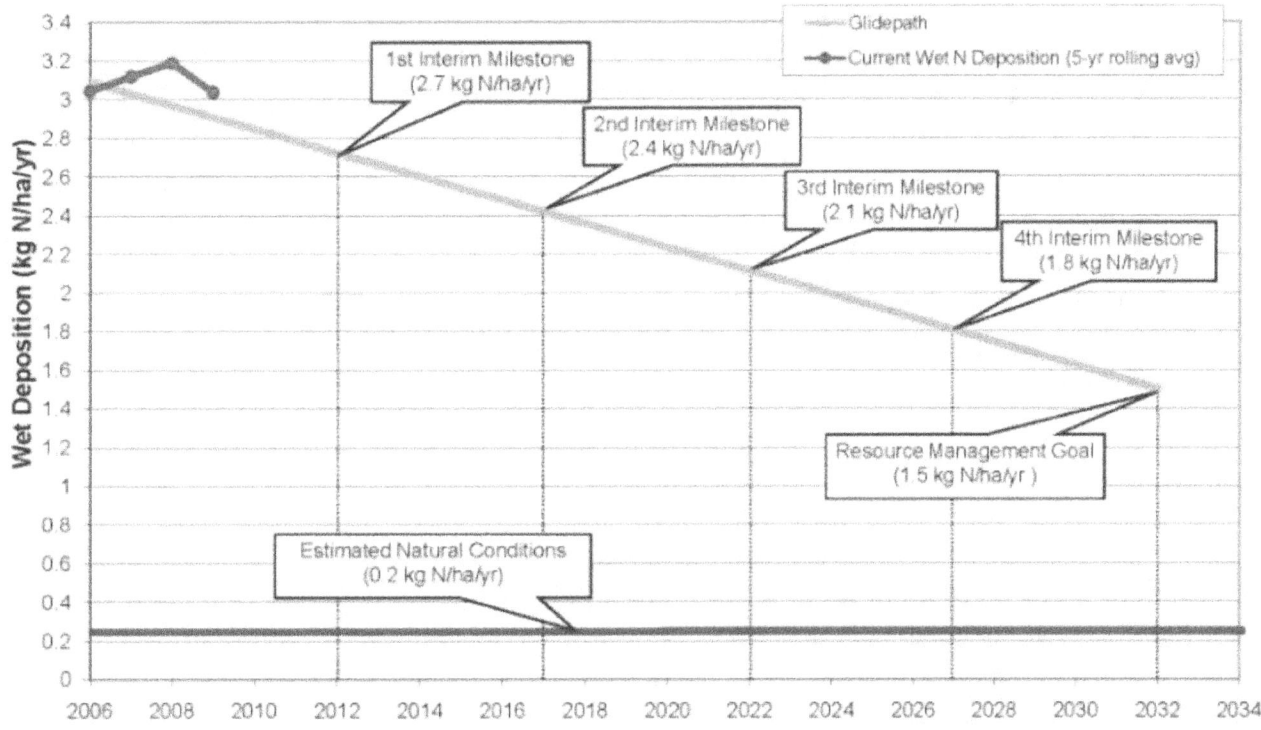

Figure 1. Glidepath and current wet nitrogen deposition at Loch Vale in Rocky Mountain NP.

NADP/NTN quality assurance programs have estimated uncertainty in the measurements by operating two co-located sites annually within the NADP/NTN network since 1986 (Wetherbee et al. 2005). These sites are typically rotated annually to provide more geographical coverage. Only three of the sites have been located in western high elevation ecosystems. The data collected at the new co-located site at Loch Vale (installation occurred in fall 2009) will be used to estimate site-specific uncertainty in the measurements and will provide three full years of data before 2013 when the MOU agencies will assess the available data to determine whether the first interim milestone has been achieved.

Figure 2 shows the annual and 5 year rolling average of wet nitrogen deposition at the Loch Vale NADP/NTN site from 1984 to 2009. Annual precipitation and the long-term average precipitation (1984–2009) are also shown. Wet nitrogen deposition increased in the 1990s during a period of above average precipitation. However, wet nitrogen deposition has exhibited less variability since then, even as Colorado experienced an extended period of drought starting in 1998. This is because concentrations of nitrogen in precipitation increased whereas precipitation amount decreased. Annual N deposition in and after 1993 appears to vary less given changes in annual precipitation prior to 1993. In 2009, precipitation amount was well above average for the first time in 12 years. Figure 2 also shows that annual deposition has varied around the first interim milestone (2.7 kg N/ha/yr) during the past decade, including in 2009 when annual deposition was 2.8 kg N/ha/yr.

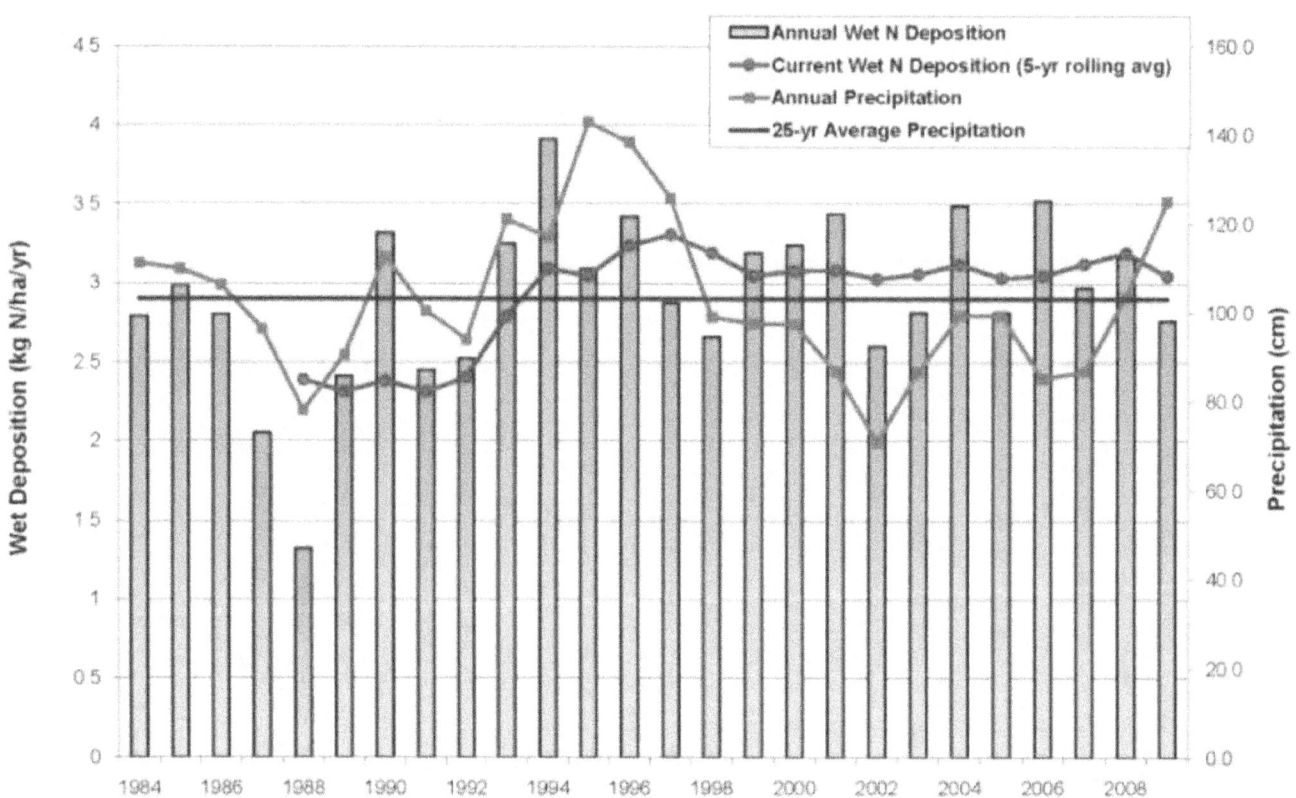

Figure 2. Wet nitrogen deposition and precipitation at Loch Vale in Rocky Mountain NP.

5.2. Long-term trends analyses for Rocky Mountain NP and other regional sites

These analyses show whether changes in nitrogen in precipitation are significant over the period of record. The NPS began monitoring precipitation chemistry at Loch Vale in 1983, so the period of record is 25 years. Statistical trends on several different parameters will provide information on how nitrogen has changed over time in order to evaluate whether nitrogen inputs to park ecosystems are either increasing, decreasing, or stable.

The parameters include wet nitrogen (N) deposition (kg N/ha/yr), precipitation-weighted mean nitrate (NO_3^-) and ammonium (NH_4^+) concentrations ($\mu eq/L$), and precipitation (cm). Each parameter provides different information. Trends analyses on deposition data provide information that is ecologically relevant and relative to the RMG for RMNP. Trends analyses on concentrations provide information on air quality at individual sites and allow for comparison among sites, with less influence due to precipitation amount.

Long-term trends were determined by the Seasonal Kendall Test (SKT). The SKT was developed by the U.S. Geological Survey in the 1980s to analyze surface-water quality throughout the U.S. (Hirsch et al. 1982). Since then, it has become one of the most frequently used tests to determine trends in environmental data (Helsel et al. 2006). Examples of SKT used to determine trends in atmospheric deposition data include Lehmann et al. (2005) and Ingersoll et al. (2008). The SKT is a non-parametric statistical test that is capable of detecting monotonic trends in data sets despite strong seasonality, missing data, and non-normal data distributions.

In order to compare data from Loch Vale with other sites exposed to similar Front Range emissions, three NADP/NTN sites located outside of the park and the two NADP/NTN sites that are located within RMNP are included in the analyses. These additional sites provide regional context and are listed in Table 1 and shown in Figure 3. Niwot Saddle and Sugarloaf complement each other as high elevation and low-elevation monitoring sites, just like Loch Vale and Beaver Meadows in RMNP. Pawnee is at a much lower elevation.

Table 1. NADP/NTN sites in and near Rocky Mountain NP.

Site Name	NADP/NTN Site ID	Period of Record	Elevation	Distance to Loch Vale
Loch Vale (RMNP)	CO98	26 yrs	3,159 m (10,364 ft)	0
Beaver Meadows (RMNP)	CO19	30 yrs	2,490 m (8,169 ft)	11 km (6.8 mi)
Niwot Saddle	CO02	26 yrs	3,520 m (11,549 ft)	26.6 km (16.5 mi)
Sugarloaf	CO94	23 yrs	2,524 m (8,281 ft)	36.2 km (22.5 mi)
Pawnee	CO22	30 yrs	1,641 m (5,384 ft)	96 km (59.7 mi)

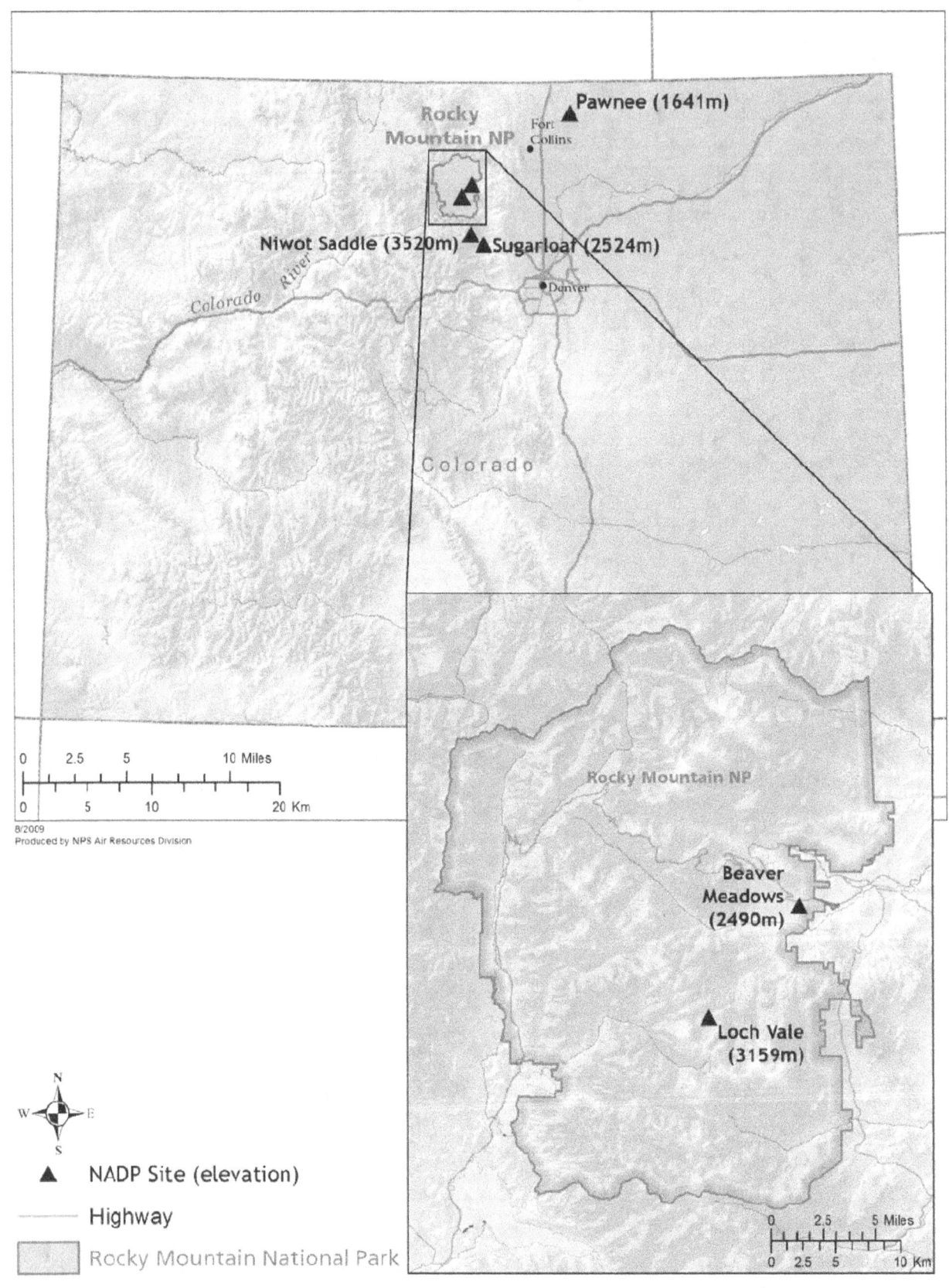

Figure 3. Map of NADP/NTN sites in and near Rocky Mountain NP.

Figure 4a–e shows the annual data for the period of record at each of the five sites for deposition, concentration, and precipitation.

Precipitation amount has varied substantially among these five Front Range sites over the period of record (22–29 years). The higher elevation sites record much more precipitation than their lower elevation counterparts. Pawnee (at the lowest elevation) records the least amount of precipitation. In 2009, precipitation at all sites increased.

In general, wet nitrogen deposition ranges from 2–4 kg N/ha/yr at all Front Range sites, except for Niwot Saddle, where deposition is much higher, mostly due to higher precipitation amounts recorded at the site (Williams et al. 1998). Annual ammonium deposition and nitrate deposition

are contributing almost equal parts to nitrogen deposition at Loch Vale, Beaver Meadows, and Sugarloaf. Nitrate deposition is higher at Niwot Saddle, and ammonium deposition is higher at Pawnee.

Nitrate and ammonium concentrations are generally in the same range among all sites, except for Pawnee, where concentrations are much higher. Nitrate concentrations are slightly higher than ammonium concentrations at all the sites, except for Pawnee where ammonium concentrations are distinctly higher. Concentrations are typically lower at the high elevation sites, where precipitation is higher. In 2009, nitrate and ammonium concentrations decreased at all sites compared to 2008, except for Pawnee where ammonium concentrations increased.

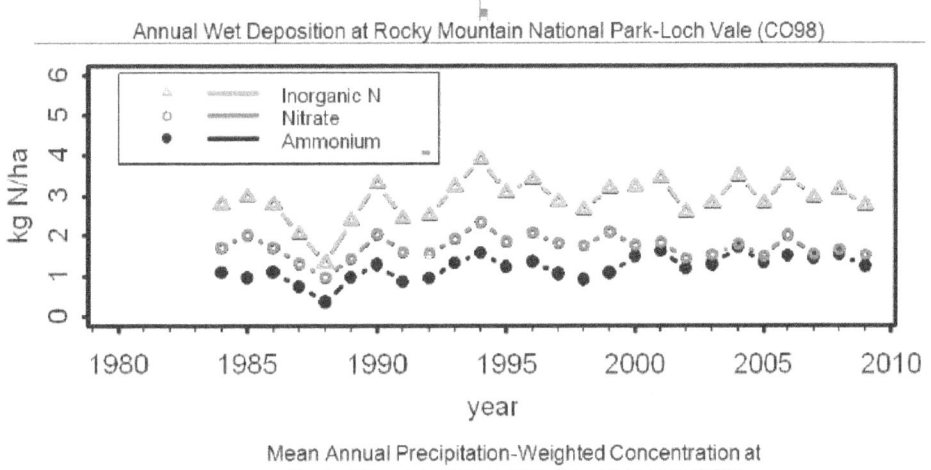

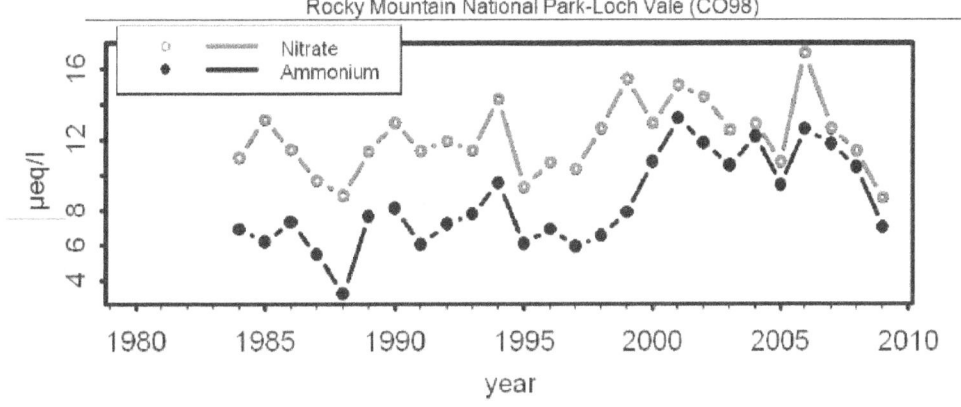

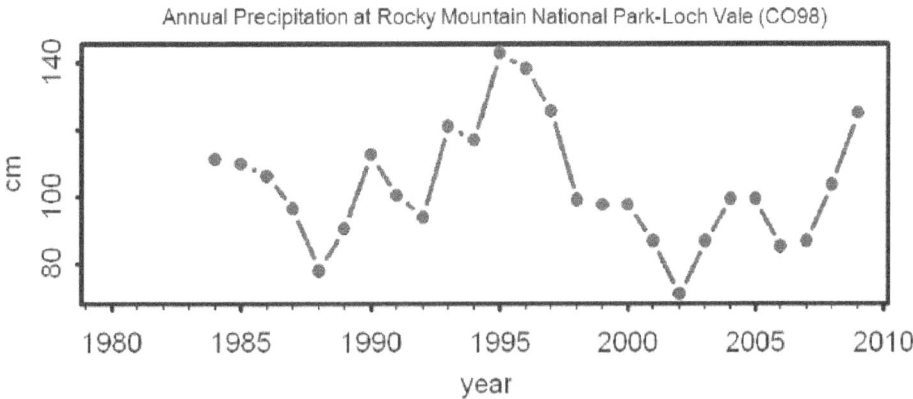

Figure 4a. Deposition, concentrations, and precipitation for Loch Vale.

Annual Wet Deposition at Rocky Mountain National Park-Beaver Meadows (CO19)

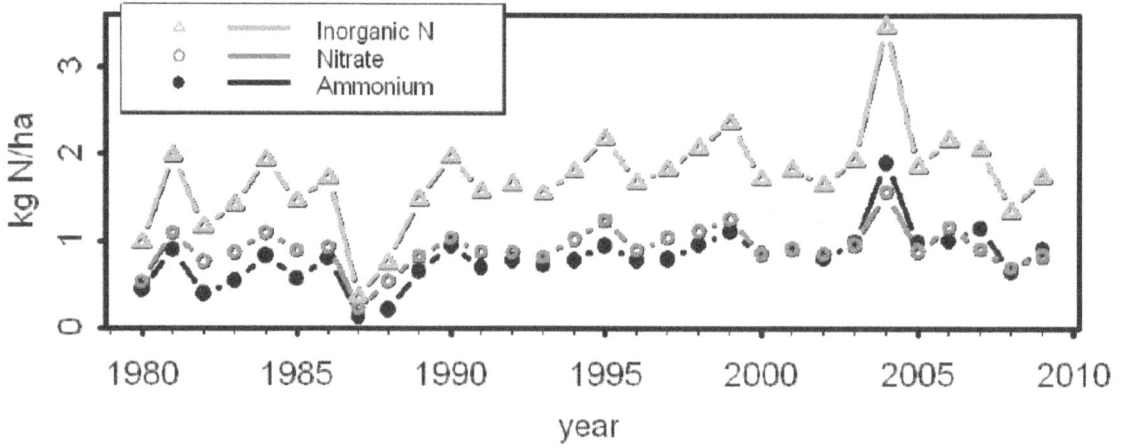

Mean Annual Precipitation-Weighted Concentration at Rocky Mountain National Park-Beaver Meadows (CO19)

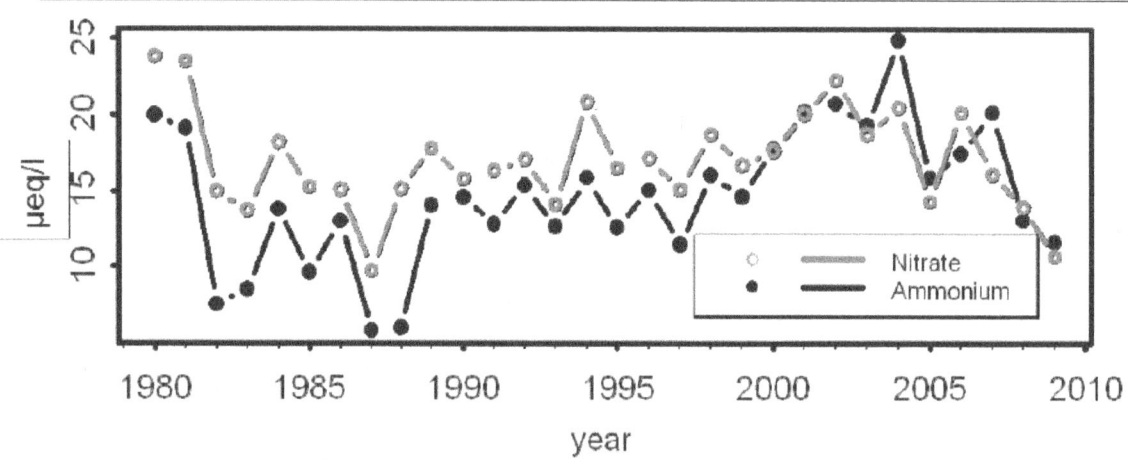

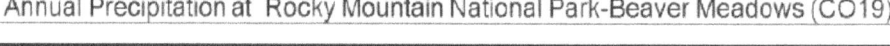

Annual Precipitation at Rocky Mountain National Park-Beaver Meadows (CO19)

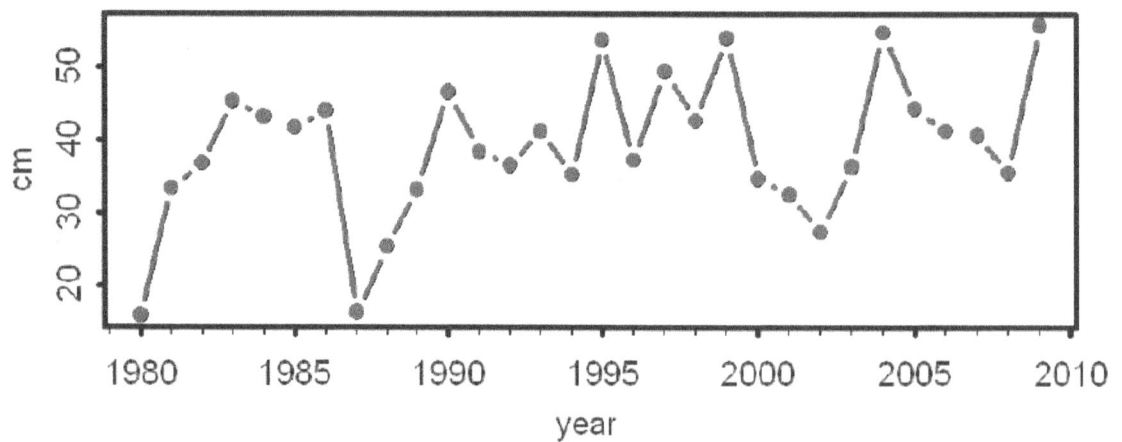

Figure 4b. Deposition, concentrations, and precipitation for Beaver Meadows.

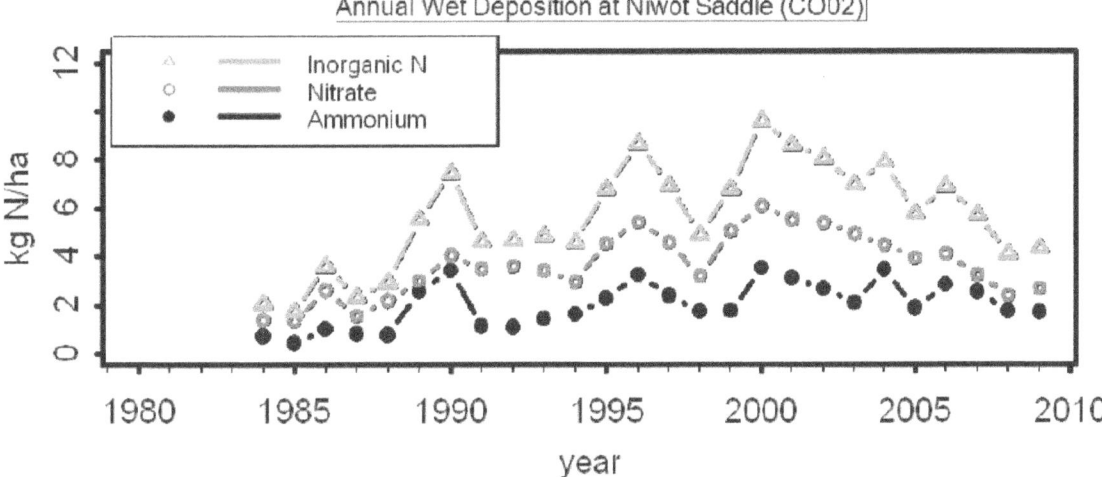

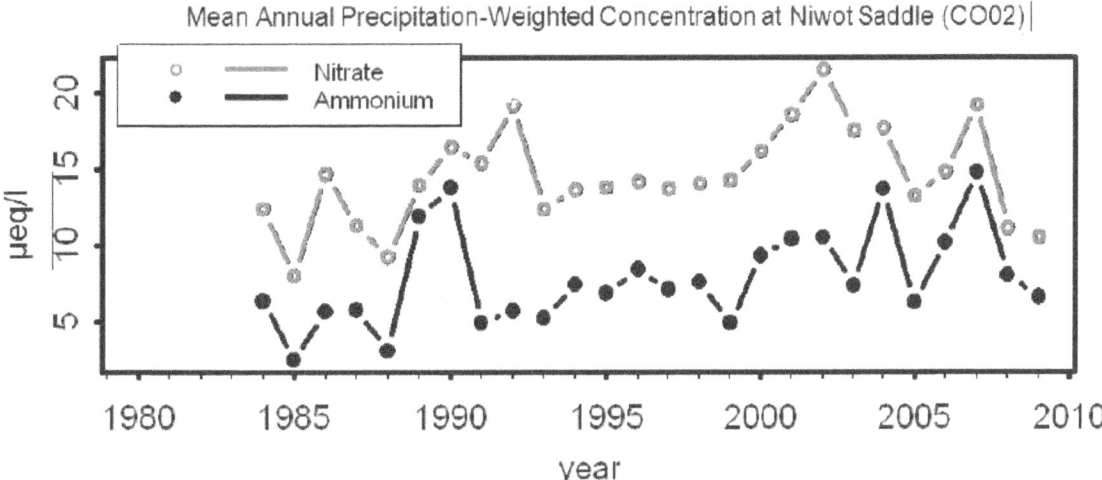

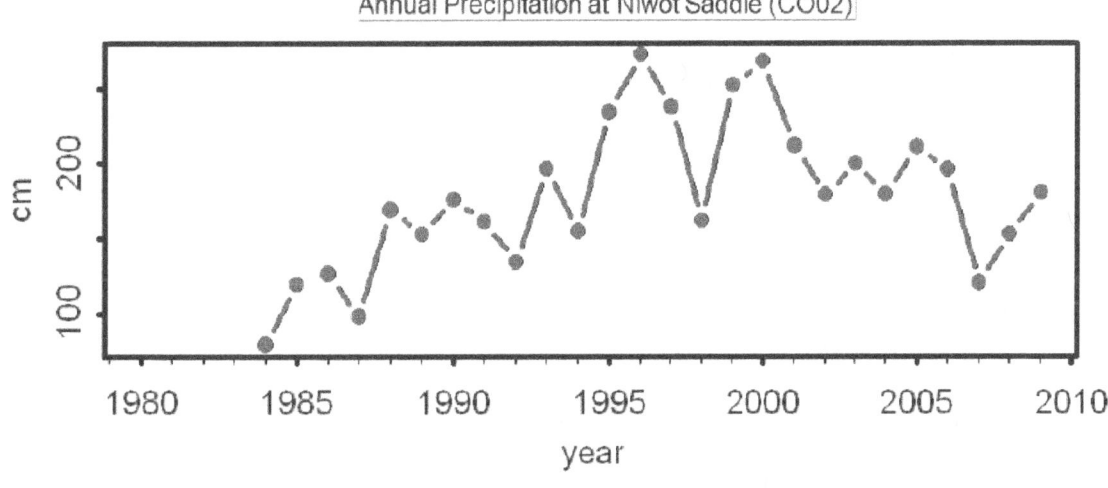

Figure 4c. Deposition, concentrations, and precipitation for Niwot Saddle.

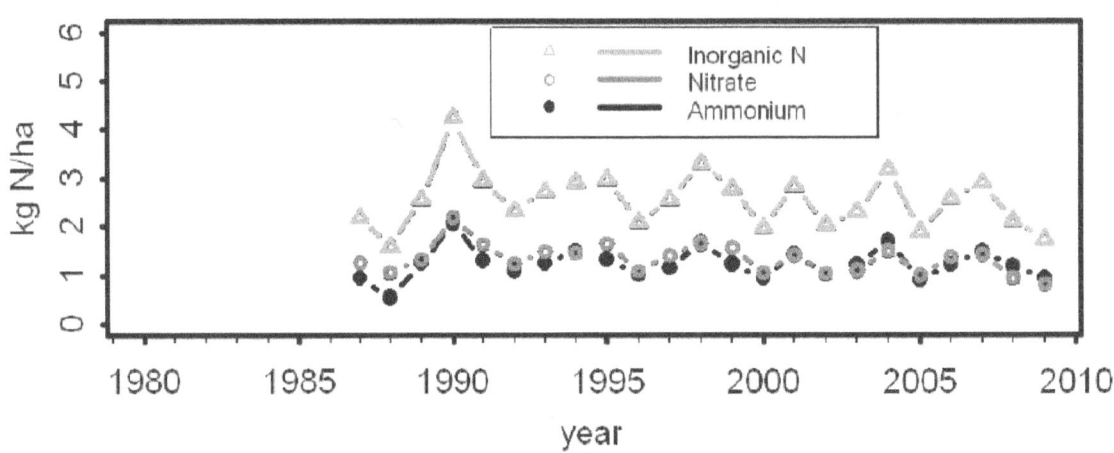

Annual Wet Deposition at Sugarloaf (CO94)

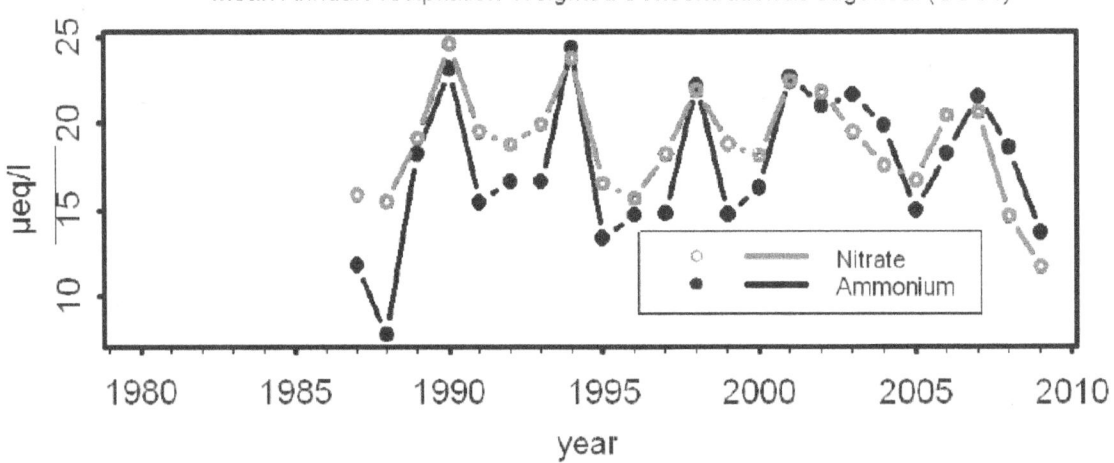

Mean Annual Precipitation-Weighted Concentration at Sugarloaf (CO94)

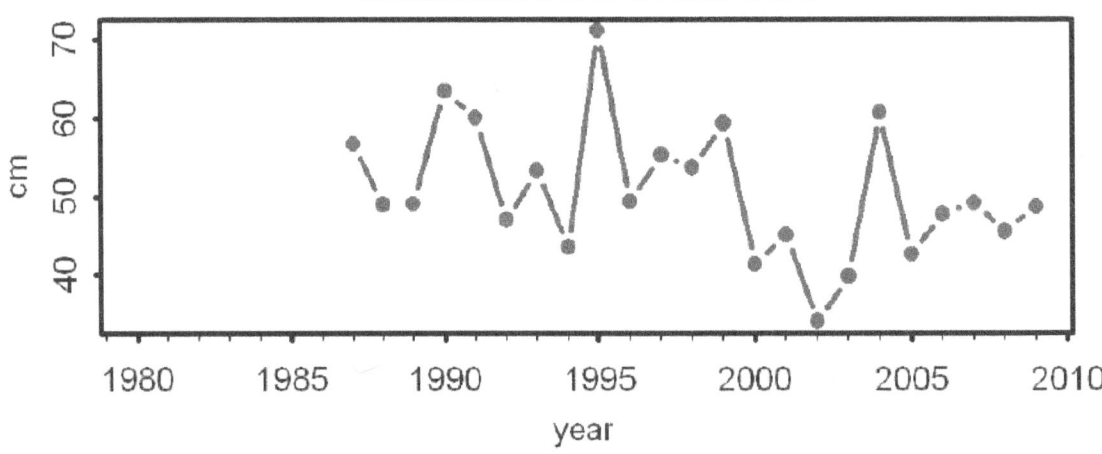

Annual Precipitation at Sugarloaf (CO94)

Figure 4d. Deposition, concentrations, and precipitation for Sugarloaf.

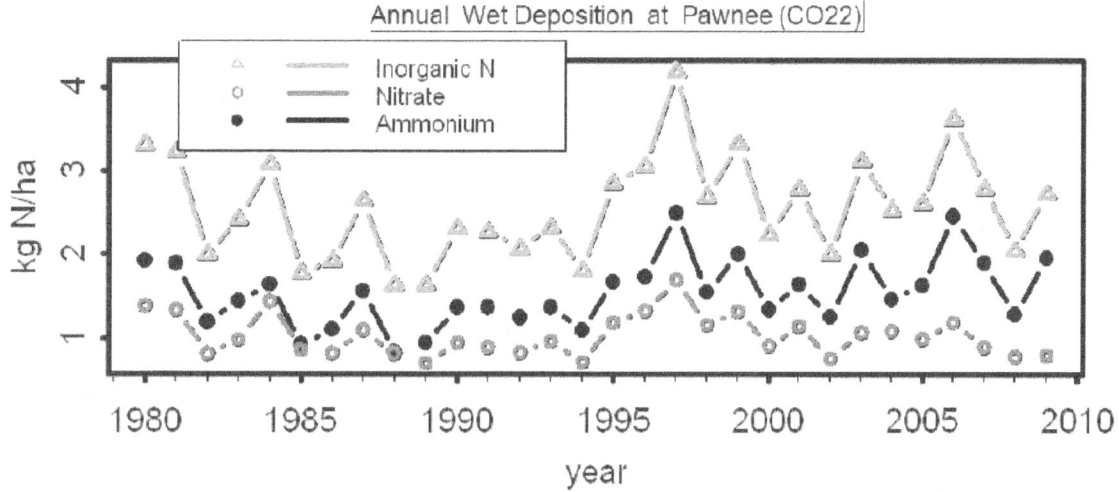

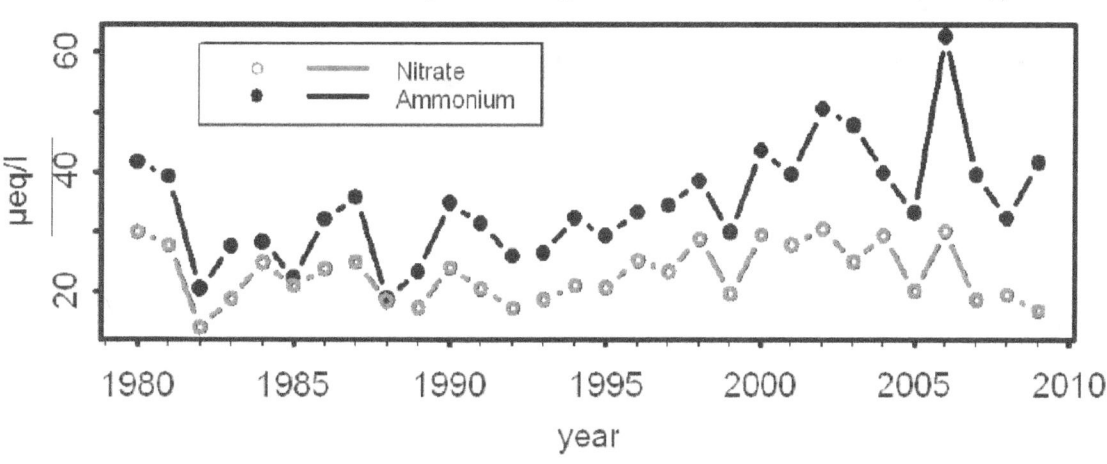

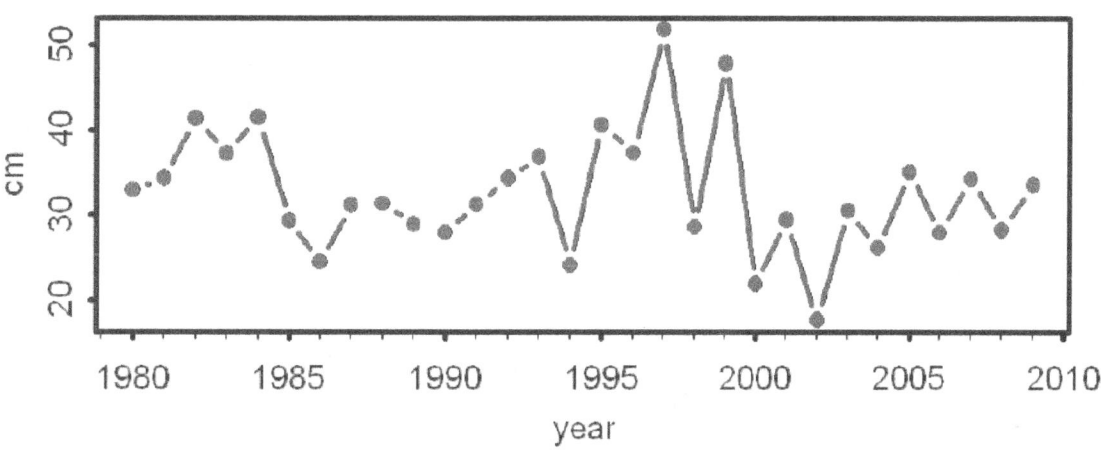

Figure 4e. Deposition, concentrations, and precipitation for Pawnee.

Table 2 shows results from the trend analysis for the entire period of record. Highlights identify the statistically significant trends, defined using a 95% confidence level (p-value ≤ 0.05). Data were obtained from the NADP/NTN website for the selected sites for the first full year of data through calendar year 2009. The data sets were reformatted and trends were computed using a computer code available through the USGS for the Kendall family of trend tests (Helsel and Frans 2006). Deposition and precipitation trends were run on annual data using the Mann-Kendall test. Concentration trends were run on quarterly data using the Seasonal Kendall Test (SKT).

A statistically significant trend in wet nitrogen deposition was not detected at Loch Vale over the period of record. The trend at Beaver Meadows in RMNP showed a significant increase (p-value = 0.031). The trend at Niwot Saddle also showed a significant increase in wet nitrogen deposition (p-value = 0.024).

The concentration of ammonium increased significantly at four of the five Front Range NADP/NTN sites over the period of record including Loch Vale, Beaver Meadows, Niwot Saddle, and Pawnee (p-values < 0.011). Concentrations of nitrate and precipitation amount were stable at all sites over the period of record.

One goal of the NDRP is to "reverse the trend of increasing nitrogen deposition at the park." The analysis of long-term trends allows us to answer the question: Has nitrogen deposition decreased at RMNP and other sites in the region? Results indicate that wet nitrogen deposition has *not* decreased at RMNP over the long term. In fact, the only significant trends detected in the region were *increasing*. The data from Loch Vale are consistent with other Front Range sites and are regionally representative. Therefore, the answer to the question is: No, nitrogen deposition has not decreased at RMNP or other sites in the region over the long term.

Table 2. Results from long-term trends over the period of record.

Wet Nitrogen Deposition				
Site Name	Start Year	Trend (kg N/ha/yr)	P-value	Significant Trends
Loch Vale	1984	0.03	0.061	–
Beaver Meadows	1981	0.02	0.031	increasing
Niwot Saddle	1985	0.15	0.024	increasing
Sugarloaf	1987	-0.02	0.259	–
Pawnee	1980	0.01	0.372	–
Ammonium Precipitation-weighted Mean Concentrations				
Site Name	Start Year	Trend (µeq/L/yr)	P-value	Significant Trends
Loch Vale	1984	0.16	0.002	increasing
Beaver Meadows	1981	0.24	0.001	increasing
Niwot Saddle	1985	0.14	0.011	increasing
Sugarloaf	1987	0.20	0.071	–
Pawnee	1980	0.45	0.005	increasing
Nitrate Precipitation-weighted Mean Concentrations				
Site Name	Start Year	Trend (µeq/L/yr)	P-value	Significant Trends
Loch Vale	1984	0.06	0.267	–
Beaver Meadows	1981	-0.02	0.985	–
Niwot Saddle	1985	0.16	0.118	–
Sugarloaf	1987	-0.01	0.949	–
Pawnee	1980	0.03	0.795	–
Precipitation				
Site Name	Start Year	Trend (cm/yr)	P-value	Significant Trends
Loch Vale	1984	-0.33	0.453	–
Beaver Meadows	1981	0.22	0.159	–
Niwot Saddle	1985	2.79	0.088	–
Sugarloaf	1987	-0.47	0.080	–
Pawnee	1980	-0.14	0.225	–

5.3. Short-term trends analyses for Rocky Mountain NP and other regional sites

These analyses show how nitrogen in precipitation has changed over a more recent period of time, which is more relevant to recent changes in emissions. Trend analyses were run using the same parameters but over two shorter time periods: 5 and 7 years, 2005–2009 and 2003–2009, respectively. Because trends are more difficult to detect statistically using smaller data sets, the regional Kendall test (RKT) was also used to determine regional trends for all Front Range sites for the 5 and 7 year time periods (Helsel and Frans 2006). In contrast to the SKT, where trends are determined for each individual site, the RKT analysis groups the sites together. Table 3 shows the results of the trend analysis for the individual sites over the shorter time periods, and Table 4 shows the results of the regional analyses. Highlights identify the statistically significant trends (p-value ≤ 0.05).

Table 3. Trend results for 5 year (2005–2009) and 7 year (2003–2009) time periods.

Wet Nitrogen Deposition

Site Name	5 year			7 year		
	Trend (kg N/ha/yr)	P-value	Significant Trends	Trend (kg N/ha/yr)	P-value	Significant Trends
Loch Vale	-0.06	0.806	–	-0.08	0.879	–
Beaver Meadows	-0.18	0.462	–	-0.12	0.229	–
Niwot Saddle	-0.84	0.221	–	-0.58	0.035	decreasing
Sugarloaf	-0.06	1.000	–	-0.09	0.367	–
Pawnee	-0.38	0.806	–	-0.06	0.763	–

Ammonium Precipitation-weighted Mean Concentrations

Site Name	5 year			7 year		
	Trend (µeq/L/yr)	P-value	Significant Trends	Trend (µeq/L/yr)	P-value	Significant Trends
Loch Vale	0.03	1.000	–	-0.35	0.546	–
Beaver Meadows	-0.77	0.391	–	-0.91	0.050	decreasing
Niwot Saddle	-0.13	0.713	–	-0.27	0.451	–
Sugarloaf	0.03	0.902	–	-0.56	0.599	–
Pawnee	-3.14	0.066	–	-3.15	0.042	decreasing

Nitrate Precipitation-weighted Mean Concentrations

Site Name	5 year			7 year		
	Trend (µeq/L/yr)	P-value	Significant Trends	Trend (µeq/L/yr)	P-value	Significant Trends
Loch Vale	-0.63	0.540	–	-0.20	0.408	–
Beaver Meadows	-1.31	0.177	–	-1.06	0.029	decreasing
Niwot Saddle	-2.26	0.111	–	-1.37	0.029	decreasing
Sugarloaf	-1.81	0.066	–	-0.78	0.201	–
Pawnee	-1.75	0.177	–	-1.82	0.009	decreasing

Precipitation

Site Name	5 year			7 year		
	Trend (cm/yr)	P-value	Significant Trends	Trend (cm/yr)	P-value	Significant Trends
Loch Vale	7.90	0.220	–	3.30	0.230	–
Beaver Meadows	0.22	1.000	–	-0.2 9	1.000	–
Niwot Saddle	5.23	0.462	–	-7.09	0.739	–
Sugarloaf	0.78	1.000	–	0.10	1.000	–
Pawnee	-0.59	0.221	–	-0.04	1.000	–

Wet nitrogen deposition at RMNP has not significantly decreased at Loch Vale or Beaver Meadows over the past 5 or 7 years. Wet nitrogen deposition has significantly decreased at Niwot Saddle over the 7 year time period (p-value = 0.035). Ammonium concentrations significantly decreased at Beaver Meadows (p-value = 0.050) and Pawnee (p-value = 0.042) over the 7 year time period. Three sites showed a significant decrease in nitrate concentrations in the 7 year time period (p-values < 0.029). No significant trends were detected at the 5 year time period. Irrespective of significance, trend slope estimates were predominately decreasing for nitrogen deposition, and ammonium and nitrate concentrations for both the 5 and 7 year time periods. There were no significant trends in precipitation amount.

The RKT detected a significant regional decrease in wet nitrogen deposition and in ammonium and nitrate concentrations in the past 7 year time period (Table 4). All five sites have negative slopes in wet nitrogen deposition, and ammonium and nitrate concentrations in the past 7 years (Table 3). This consistency was confirmed by the significant regional trends for these parameters. A significant regional decrease was also found in nitrate concentrations for the 5-year time period. There were no significant trends in precipitation amount.

The analysis of short-term trends allows us to answer the question: Has nitrogen deposition recently decreased at RMNP and at other sites in the region? The answer to the question is: Yes, nitrogen deposition has recently decreased at some sites, but not at the RMNP Loch Vale site. Regional decreases were detected in wet nitrogen deposition, and ammonium and nitrate concentrations at the 7 year time scale. Only nitrate concentrations decreased at the 5 year time scale.

6. Summary

Determination of the success or failure of the goals of the NDRP will be determined by the weight of evidence, including but not limited to the following analyses:

1. Assessment of progress along the glidepath. Is current wet nitrogen deposition in RMNP on or below the glidepath? Wet nitrogen deposition is not on or below the glidepath in 2009.
2. Long-term trend analyses for RMNP and other regional sites. Has nitrogen deposition decreased at RMNP and other sites in the region in the long term? Nitrogen deposition has not decreased at RMNP or other sites in the region over the long term.
3. Short-term trends analyses for RMNP and other regional sites. Has nitrogen deposition recently decreased at RMNP and at other sites in the region? Nitrogen deposition has recently decreased in the region, but not at the RMNP Loch Vale site.

Table 4. Regional Kendall Test results for shorter-term trends (2005–2009 and 2003–2009) for five Front Range sites.

Measurement Type	5 year			7 year		
	Trend	P-value	Significant Trends	Trend	P-value	Significant Trends
Wet nitrogen deposition (kg N/ha/yr)	-0.18	0.123	–	-0.16	0.018	decreasing
Ammonium concentration (µeq/L/yr)	-0.39	0.188	–	-0.57	0.006	decreasing
Nitrate concentration (µeq/L/yr)	-1.41	0.001	decreasing	-1.15	<0.001	decreasing
Precipitation (cm/yr)	0.65	0.742	–	0.13	0.788	–

References

Baron, J. S. 2006. Hindcasting nitrogen deposition to determine an ecological critical load. *Ecological Applications* 16(2): 433–439.

Dentener, F. J. 2001. Personal communication with Tamara Blett, National Park Service. Globally modeled nitrogen maps for 1860.

Galloway, J. N., W. H. Schlesinger, H. Levy II, A. Michaels, J.L. Schnoor. 1995. Nitrogen fixation: Anthropogenic enhancement — environmental response. *Global Biogeochemical Cycles* 9(2): 235–252.

Galloway, J. N., W. C. Keene, G. E. Likens. 1996. Processes controlling the composition of precipitation at a remote Southern hemisphere location: Torres del Paine National Park, Chile. *Journal of Geophysical Research* 101(D3): 6883–6897.

Helsel, D. R. and L. M. Frans. 2006. Regional Kendall test for trend. *Environmental Science & Technology* 40(13): 4066–4073.

Helsel, D. R., D. K. Mueller, J. R. Slack. 2006. Computer program for the Kendall family of trend tests. U.S. Geological Survey Scientific Investigations Report 2005–5275, 4 pp. [http://pubs.usgs.gov/sir/2005/5275/pdf/sir2005-5275.pdf].

Hirsch, R. M., J. R. Slack, R. A. Smith. 1982. Techniques of trend analysis for monthly water quality data. *Water Resources Research* 18 107–121.

Ingersoll, G. P., M. A. Mast, D. H. Campbell, D. W. Clow, L. Nanus, J. T. Turk. 2008. Trends in snowpack chemistry and comparison to National Atmospheric Deposition Program results for the Rocky Mountains, U.S., 1993–2004. *Atmospheric Environment* 42: 6098–6113.

Ingersoll, G. P. 2010. Personal communication. U.S. Geologic Survey.

Lehmann, C. M. B., V. C. Bowersox, S. M. Larson. 2005. Spatial and temporal trends of precipitation chemistry in the United States, 1985–2002. *Environmental Pollution* 135: 347–361.

Wetherbee, G. A., N.E. Latysh, J. D. Gordon. 2005. Spatial and temporal variability of the overall error of National Atmospheric Deposition Program measurements determined by the USGS collocated-sampler program, water years 1989–2001. *Environmental Pollution* 135: 407–418.

Williams, M.W., T. Bardsley, M. Rikkers. 1998. Overestimation of snow depth and inorganic nitrogen wetfall using NADP data, Niwot Ridge, Colorado. *Atmospheric Environment* 32: 3827–3833.

Appendix A: A History of the Loch Vale NAPD/NTN Monitoring Site

The Loch Vale NADP/NTN site was established in the summer of 1983, when the original precipitation collector and Belfort rain gage were installed. In 2006, after extensive laboratory and field testing, the NADP/NTN approved two new electronic rain gages, the Hach Ott Pluvio and the ETI NOAH IV. During the summer of 2007, a NOAH IV rain gage was installed at the Loch Vale site. The original Belfort and the new NOAH IV operated side-by-side for two years (2008 and 2009) so that differences in recorded precipitation could be adequately characterized (discussion in Appendix B). Precipitation values posted on the NADP/NTN website (http://nadp.sws.uiuc.edu) beginning in 2008 are from the NOAH IV rain gage. The original Belfort rain gage was removed during the summer of 2010 in an effort to keep the monitoring site footprint to a minimum in accordance with the park's Wilderness Designation. The current site consists of two precipitation collectors and two NOAH IV rain gages.

Loch Vale NADP/NTN monitoring site history.

Date	Event
Summer 1983	Site installed with original precipitation collector and original Belfort rain gage (NADP/NTN site CO98).
Summer 2007	NOAH IV rain gage added (intended to replace Belfort rain gage, once differences were documented).
Fall 2009	Co-located site (NADP/NTN site CO89) and telemetry installed, solar power and storage increased.
Summer 2010	Belfort rain gage removed.

Appendix B: Comparison of the Belfort and NOAH IV Rain Gages

The table below shows how the amount of precipitation measured by the original Belfort and the new NOAH IV compared on days that both gages were operating in 2008 and 2009. The NOAH IV rain gage recorded 6.4 and 6.5% more precipitation than the Belfort during 2008 and 2009, respectively. The NOAH IV is a more sensitive gage that is capable of catching more light and blowing snow. The NADP/NTN External QA Program has compared co-located Belfort rain gages at many sites across the network and reports that the variability between two of the same Belfort rain gages is approximately ± 5%. The approximately 6.5% difference between the two different rain gages is considered to be consistent with other gages, and a relatively small difference. Therefore, a correction was not applied to the precipitation data in this report.

However, the small increase in precipitation affects annual deposition and potentially the 5 year average that is compared to the glidepath. In order to determine the significance of the increase, annual deposition at Loch Vale and the 5 year average were calculated based on a 6.45% decrease in precipitation for 2008 and 2009 (decrease, because the precipitation amounts reported on the NADP/NTN website in 2008 and 2009 are from the NOAH IV rain gage). Annual deposition decreased from 3.16 to 2.96 and from 2.76 to 2.58 kg N/ha/yr in 2008 and 2009, respectively.

The 5 year rolling averages for deposition were calculated with 6.45% less precipitation and are compared to deposition calculated with precipitation from the NOAH IV in the table below. The results in the table show there are small differences in the 5 year averages but that when the values are rounded to 2-significant digits, which is how deposition is reported, a 6.45% increase in precipitation makes no difference in the values that are compared to the glidepath.

Comparison of the Belfort and NOAH IV rain gages.

Year	Data Available for Both Gages (days)	Measured Precipitation (cm)		% Difference (NOAH IV - Belfort)
		Belfort	NOAH IV	
2008	322	88.44	94.13	6.4%
2009	326	109.47	116.61	6.5%

5 year average nitrogen deposition.

5 Year Period	Deposition (Precipitation from NOAH IV)	With 6.45% Less Precipitation	Rounded to 2-Significant Digits
2004-2008	3.19	3.15	3.2
2005-2009	3.04	2.97	3.0

Appendix C: Explanation of NADP/NTN Terms and Calculations

The NADP/NTN collects weekly precipitation samples and records precipitation amount. Concentrations of sulfate, nitrate, chloride, ammonium, and base cations are determined by laboratory analysis and reported in units of mg/L. Hydrogen ion is reported as pH. Weekly precipitation samples are aggregated into precipitation-weighted mean concentrations for monthly, seasonal, and annual time periods by using Equation (1).

$$\overline{C}_{pptwt} = \frac{\sum_{i=1}^{n} \left(C_{w,i} \times P_{w,i} \right)}{\sum_{i=1}^{n} P_{w,i}} \qquad \text{(Eq. 1)}$$

where:

$\overline{C}_{ppt\,wt}$ = precipitation-weighted mean concentration, mg/L

$C_{w,i}$ = precipitation concentration for individual event, mg/L

$P_{w,i}$ = Precipitation depth for individual event, cm

n = number of events

Precipitation-weighted mean concentrations are used in order to simulate having one composite sample over the time period of interest. For example, a precipitation-weighted mean concentration for one year (or month or season) is equivalent to adding all of the weekly samples together into one sample and then determining the concentration of ions in that sample.

Example: sample concentration and precipitation amount.

Sample	Concentration	Precipitation Amount
1	15 mg/L	1 cm
2	5 mg/L	6 cm

A precipitation-weighted mean concentration is more representative of the average concentration of the majority of the precipitation. In the above example, the precipitation-weighted mean concentration is 6.43 mg/L[(15 x 1 + 5x6)/(1+6)] and is more heavily influenced by the larger precipitation event, whereas an arithmetic mean is 10 mg/L.

Precipitation concentrations can also be presented in terms of microequivalents per liter (µeq/L). An equivalent is defined as a mass of an element that can combine with

1 gram of hydrogen in a chemical reaction. It is a way of normalizing for ionic charge. Nitrate ion has one negative charge (NO_3^-) and ammonium has one positive charge (NH_4^+), once converted to µeq/L the ion concentrations can be compared to each other. Concentrations in mg/L are converted to µeq/L by using the factors listed in following table.

Conversion factors for ion concentrations, mg/L to µeq/L.

Ion	Conversion Factor
Ammonium	1 mg/L = 55.4371 µeq/L
Nitrate	1 mg/L = 16.12776 µeq/L

Wet deposition is calculated by multiplying the precipitation-weighted mean concentration for a period of time by the total amount of precipitation during that time (Equation 2).

$$D_w = \overline{C}_{pptwt} \times P_{TOT} \times 10^{-1} \qquad \text{(Eq. 2)}$$

where:

D_w = wet deposition, kg/ha

$\overline{C}_{ppt\,wt}$ = precipitation-weighted mean concentration, mg/L

P_{TOT} = total precipitation depth for period, cm

Nitrogen deposition is calculated by summing the nitrogen (N) from nitrate (NO_3) deposition and ammonium (NH_4) deposition as shown in (Equation 3). The conversion factors in the equation represent the molecular weight ratios of N to NH_4 and NO_3, respectively.

$$D_{IN} = \left(D_{NH_4^+} \times \frac{14.01}{18.01} \right) + \left(D_{NO_3^-} \times \frac{14.01}{62.01} \right) \qquad \text{(Eq. 3)}$$

where:

D_{IN} = wet deposition of N, kg/ha

$D_{NH_4^+}$ = wet deposition of NH_4, kg/ha

$D_{NO_3^-}$ = wet deposition of NO_3, kg/ha

The Department of the Interior protects and manages the nation's natural resources and cultural heritage; provides scientific and other information about those resources; and honors its special responsibilities to American Indians, Alaska Natives, and affiliated Island Communities.

NPS 121/109707, September 2011

www.ingramcontent.com/pod-product-compliance
Lightning Source LLC
Chambersburg PA
CBHW080352290526
45791CB00009BA/2849